## About Starters Facts

This colorful new range of information books encourages young readers to find out things for themselves. The text is graded into three reading levels — red, blue, and green. As well as providing a valuable source of reference, the books encourage further interest in the topic through activities and puzzles.

Accompanying each FACTS book is a STARTERS STORY, which uses the same topic as the starting point for an exciting story.

### Reading Consultants

Betty Root, Tutor-in-charge, Center for the Teaching of Reading, University of Reading.

Geoffrey Ivimey, Senior Lecturer in Child Development, University of London Institute of Education.

### Going to the Hospital

The publishers would like to thank Dr. Hugh Jolly and Jan Kubli, Play Co-ordinator, of the Department of Paediatrics, Charing Cross Hospital, without whose advice and assistance this book would not have been possible.

# Going to the Hospital

illustrated by
**Sara Silcock**

Starters Facts • Red 4

Emma and mommy are
at the bus stop.
They have to wait for the bus.

They are going to the hospital.
Emma has to see the doctor.

Emma has seen the doctor before.
She has asthma. Sometimes she
can't breathe very well.

When they get to the hospital
they go into a big room,
which is full of children.

There is a lady in the room.
She plays with all the children
while they wait.

The nurse asks Emma
to stand on the scales,
to find out how heavy she is.

Then the nurse measures Emma.
She has to see if Emma
has grown since her last visit.

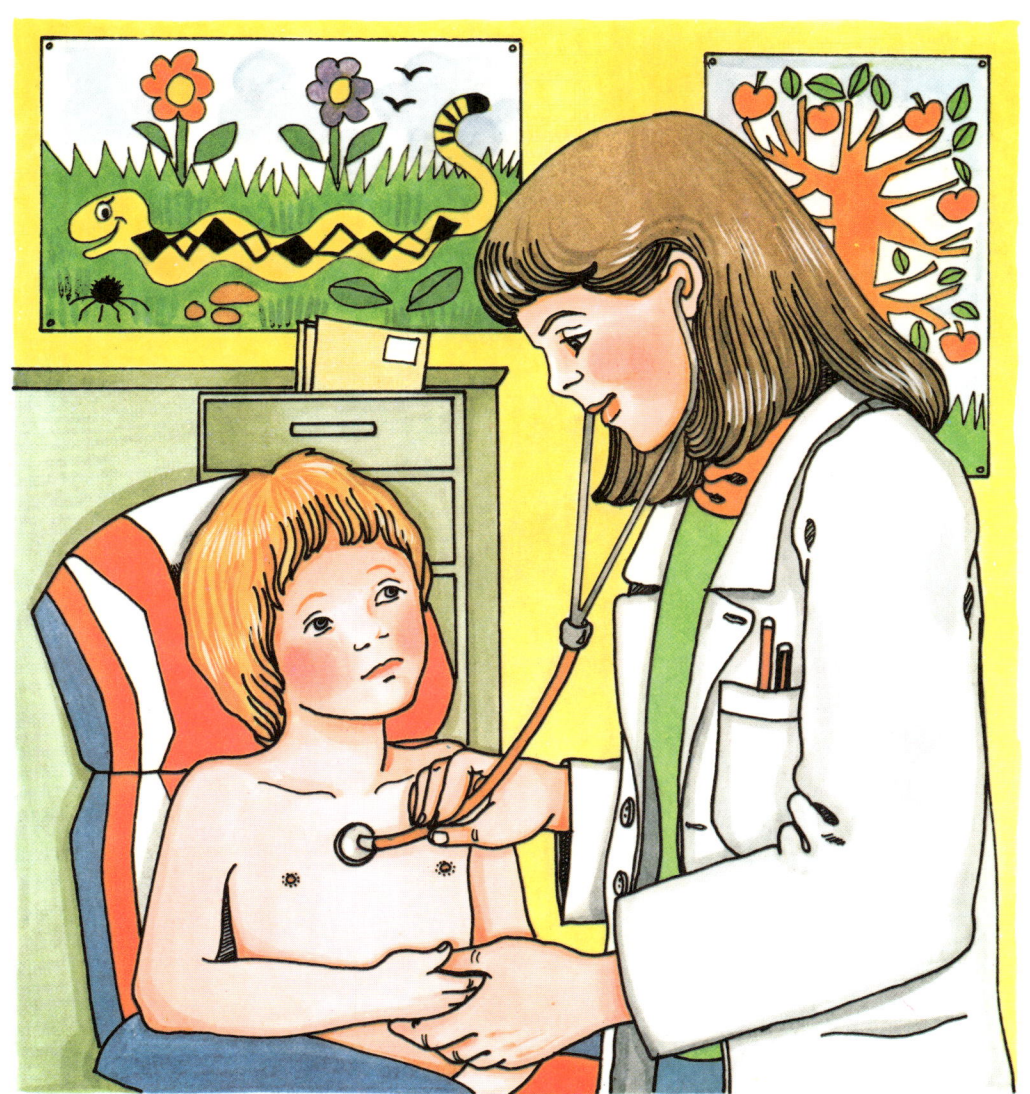

They go in to see the doctor.
The doctor listens to Emma's
chest with a stethoscope.

Emma's chest is very wheezy,
and she can't breathe very well.
She must stay in the hospital.

She goes home with mommy
to get her nightie and toys.
When they get back,
they go to the playroom.

Emma still can't breathe very well.
They nurse goes to get a machine
that will help her breathe.

The machine is full of air.
A bottle and a tube are fixed to it.
There is a spray inside the bottle,
with medicine in it.

Emma has to put a mask on, and the spray makes her feel much better.

Emma sees lots of children.
Most of them are playing, but
a few are in bed.

One boy has a broken leg.
He ran in front of a car,
and was knocked down.

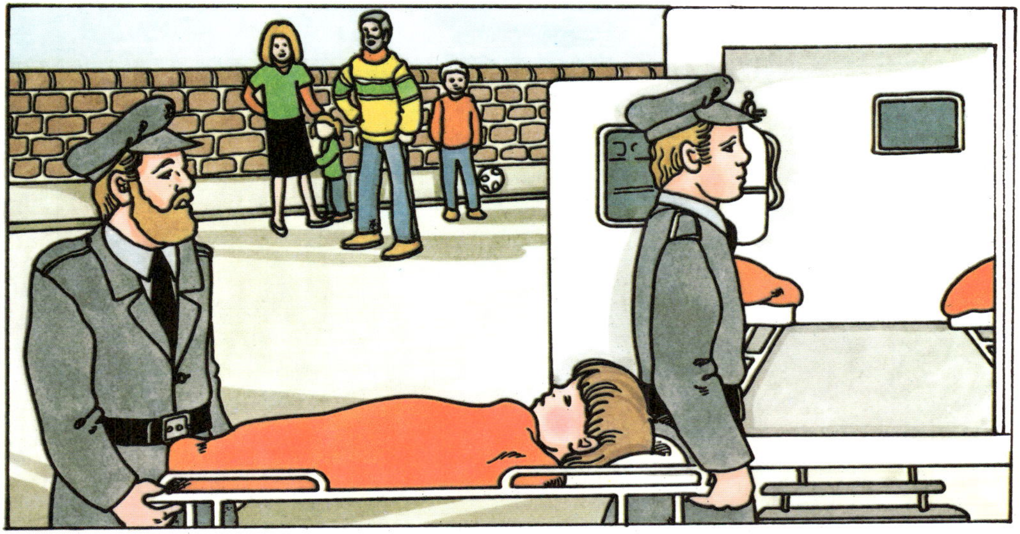

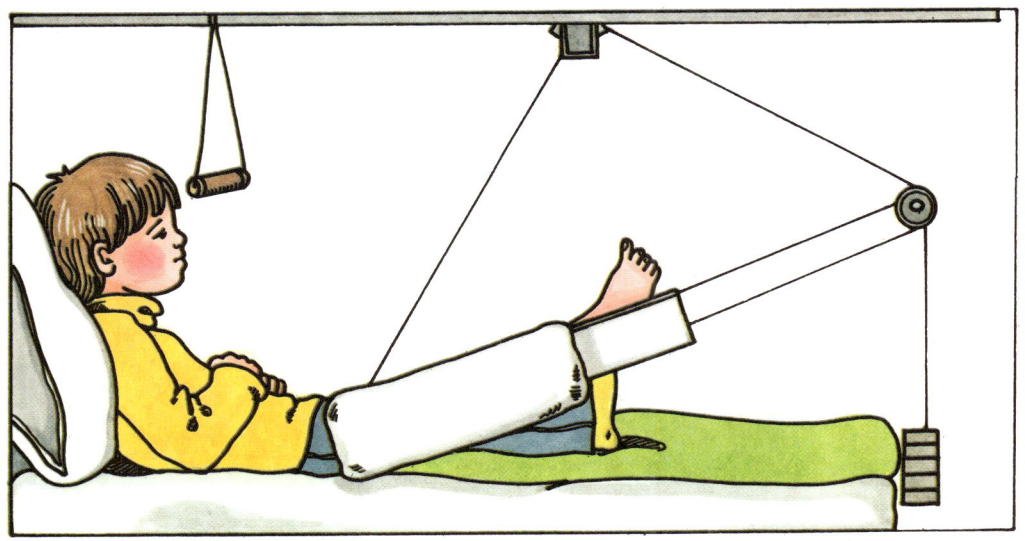

He came to the hospital by ambulance.
His broken leg is held up above
his bed to keep it straight.

There is a teacher in the playroom.
He tells Emma the names of the
pills she has to take.

There are some moms and dads playing with the children.
Emma's mother is going to stay at the hospital all night.

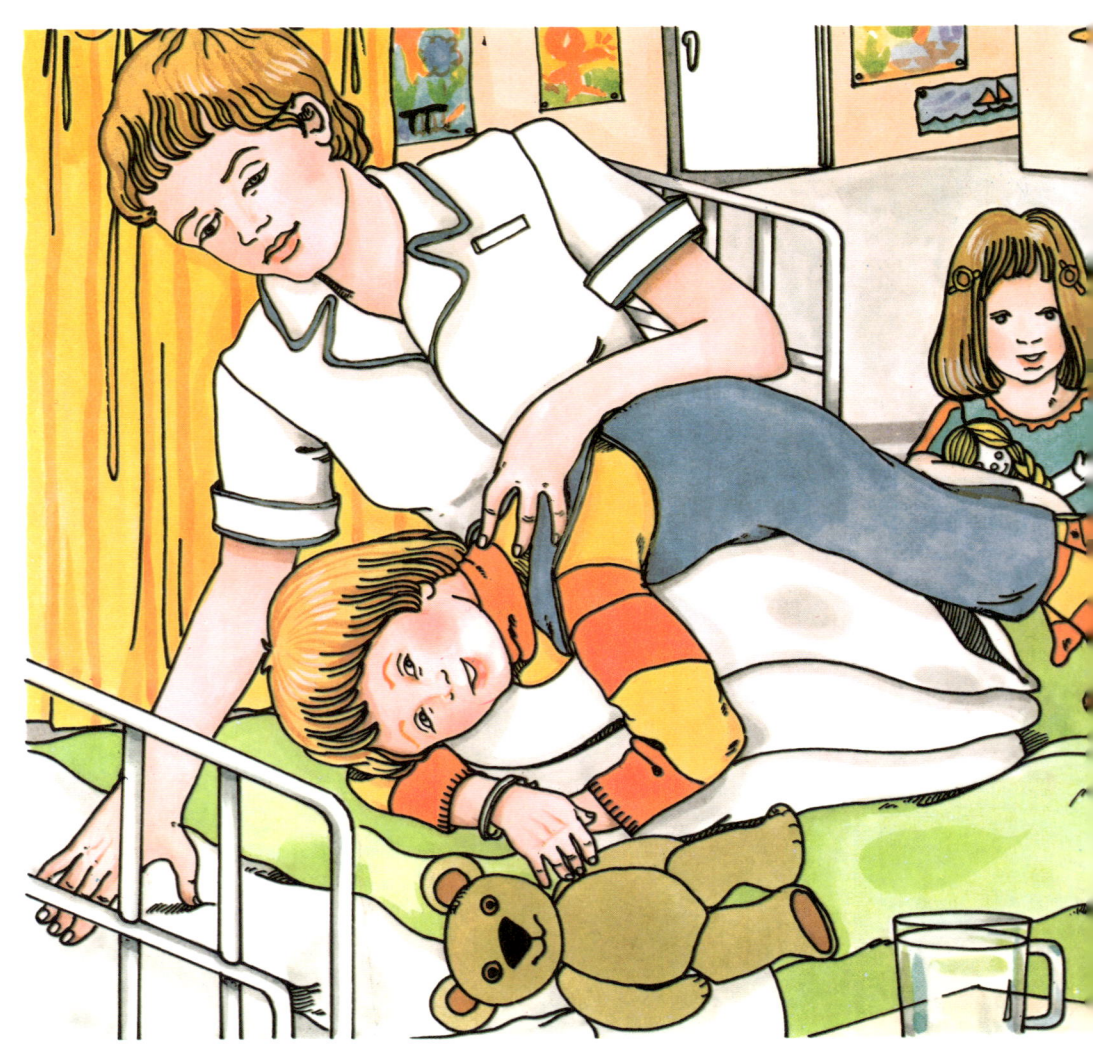

A lady comes to see Emma.
She gives people exercises
to help them get better.

She pats Emma's back
in a special way,
and mommy watches.
Emma's chest soon feels better.

She shows mommy and Emma some exercises to do at home. Emma has to take deep breaths, and then breathe out slowly.

Emma can go home the next day,
but she will have to come back again.
The doctor must be sure that
her chest is getting better.

# Hospital Activities

Make a model of a nurse.
You will need a cardboard tube,
a pipe cleaner, cotton balls,
tape, white paper, and paint.

1. Paint blue and white stripes down the tube for the nurse's dress, then paint on her face and legs.

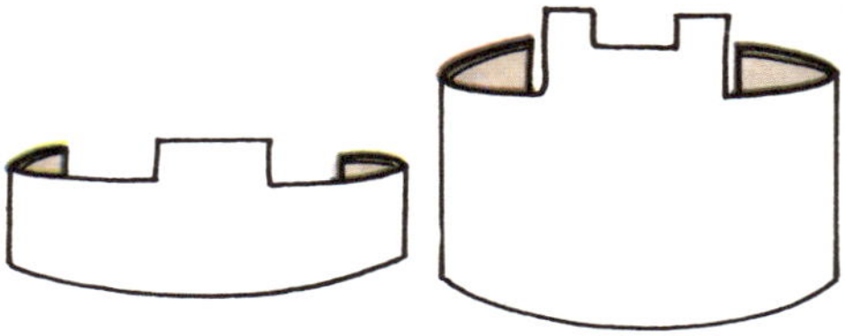

2. Cut out her cap and apron from white paper. Tape them to the tube.

3. Make holes for her arms and push the pipe cleaner through.

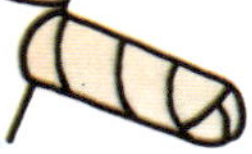

4. Wrap a cotton ball around each end of the pipe cleaner. Cover it with tape.

5. Cut out her watch and glue it to the apron.

# Hospital Quiz

Look at these pictures.
See if you can say which of them
  helps you breathe
  shows how heavy you are
  listens to your chest
  brings you to the hospital

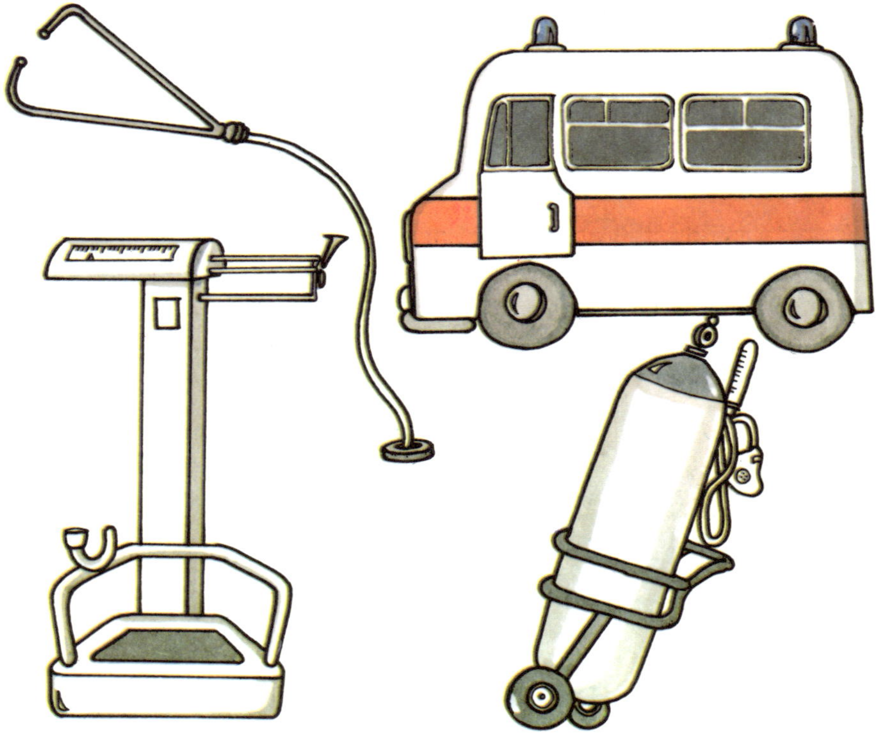

# Hospital Puzzle

The patient has lost her bed.
The doctor has lost
her stethoscope.
The nurse has lost her watch.
Can you help them find them?

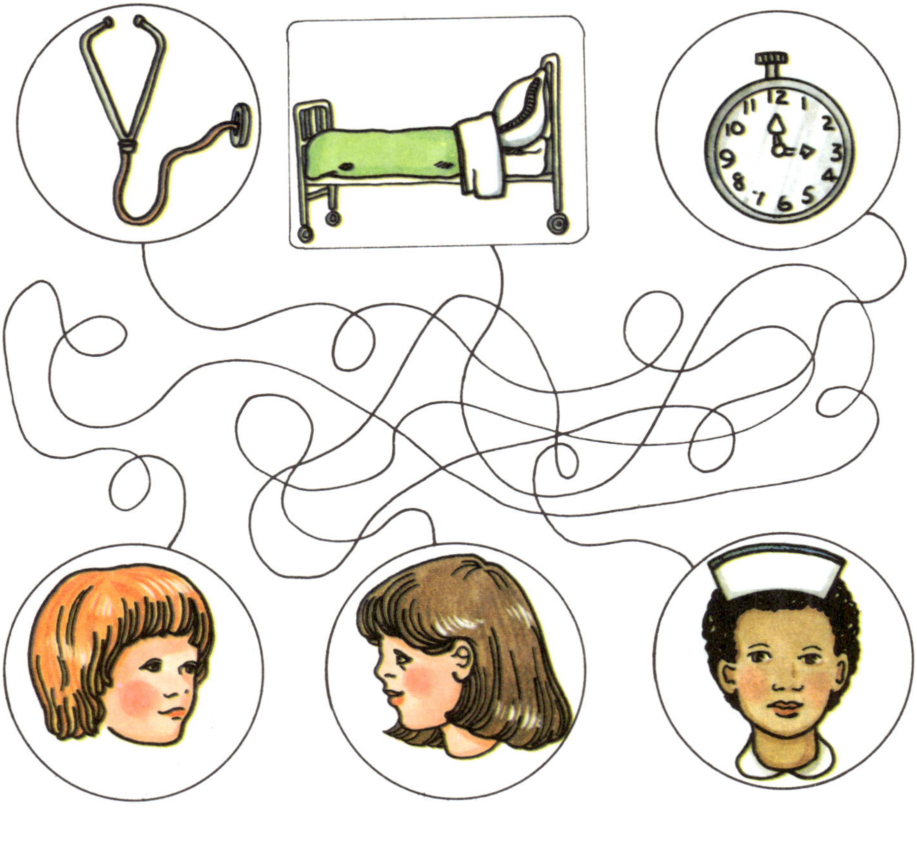

# Hospital Word List

| | |
|---|---|
| nurse page 7 | ambulance page 17 |
| scales page 7 | broken leg page 17 |
| doctor page 9 | pills page 18 |
| stethoscope page 9 | exercises page 20 |
| machine page 13 | watch page 27 |

Each information book is linked to a story in the new **Starters** program. Both kinds of book are graded into progressive reading levels — red, blue, and green. Titles in the program include:

## Starters Facts
RED 1: Going to the Zoo
RED 2: Birds
RED 3: Clowns
RED 4: Going to the Hospital
RED 5: Going to School

BLUE 1: Space Travel
BLUE 2: Cars
BLUE 3: Dinosaurs
BLUE 4: Christmas
BLUE 5: Trains

GREEN 1: Airport
GREEN 2: Moon
GREEN 3: Forts and Castles
GREEN 4: Stars
GREEN 5: Earth

## Starters Stories
RED 1: Zoo for Sale
RED 2: The Birds from Africa
RED 3: Sultan's Elephants
RED 4: Rosie's Hospital Story
RED 5: Danny's Class

BLUE 1: The Space Monster
BLUE 2: The Red Racing Car
BLUE 3: The Dinosaur's Footprint
BLUE 4: Palace of Snow
BLUE 5: Mountain Express

GREEN 1: Flight into Danger
GREEN 2: Anna and the Moon Queen
GREEN 3: The Secret Castle
GREEN 4: The Lost Starship
GREEN 5: Nuka's Tale

First published 1980 by
Macdonald Educational Ltd.,
Holywell House,
Worship Street,
London EC2

© Macdonald Educational Ltd. 1980

ISBN 0-382-06480-1
Published in the United States by
Silver Burdett Company
Morristown, New Jersey
1980 Printing

Library of Congress
Catalog Card No. 80-52526

**Editor:** Annabel McLaren
**Teacher Panel:** Susan Alston, Susan Batten, Ann Merriman, Julia Rickell, Gwen Trier
**Art Agency:** Linda Rogers Associates
**Production:** Rosemary Bishop